W9-ADH-702

EDGE BOOKS™

NATURE'S INVADERS

PESKY CRITTERS!

SQUIRRELS, RACCOONS,
AND OTHER FURRY INVADERS

BY JOAN AXELROD-CONTRADA

Consultant:
Katrina M. Dlugosch, Assistant Professor
Ecology & Evolutionary Biology

CAPSTONE PRESS
a capstone imprint

Edge Books are published by Capstone Press,
1710 Roe Crest Drive, North Mankato, Minnesota 56003
www.capstonepub.com

Library of Congress Cataloging-in-Publication Data
Axelrod-Contrada, Joan.
Pesky critters! : squirrels, raccoons, and other furry invaders / by Joan
Axelrod-Contrada.
p. cm.—(Edge books. Nature's invaders)
Summary: "A look at squirrels, raccoons, and other pesky critters, as well as what
ways to prevent unwanted visitors from invading your home"—Provided by
publisher.
Audience: 008-014.
Audience: Grades 4 to 6.
Includes bibliographical references and index.
ISBN 978-1-4765-0141-3 (library binding)
ISBN 978-1-4765-3395-7 (eBook PDF)
1. Pests—Juvenile literature. 2. Pests—Control—Juvenile literature.
3. Animal behavior—Juvenile literature. I. Title.
SB603.3.A94 2014
591.6'5—dc23   2013005606

Editorial Credits
Anthony Wacholtz, editor; Ted Williams, designer; Eric Manske, production specialist

Photo Credits
Alamy: blickwinkel/Schmidbauer, 5, Dave Bevan, 18-19, imagebroker/Ingo Schulz,
10; Dreamstime: Dohnal, 18 (inset), Renegadewanderer, 10 (inset); Shutterstock:
anatolypareev, 17, Becky Sheridan, cover (raccoon), Denise Kappa, 14 (inset),
DWPhoto, 7, Geoffrey Kuchera, 9, glenda, 27, Ivan Kuzmin, 1, James Coleman, 3
(skunk), janr34, 14-15, Jerome Whittingham, 3 (bat houses), 28, Jerry J. Davis, 6, Jodie
Richelle, cover (squirrel), 12 (bottom), KOO, 16 (inset), Kuttelvaserova Stuchelova,
cover, (tail), Newton Page, 22, Pakhnyushcha, cover (rat), PrairieEyes, 20-21, Shane
Wilson Link, 12-13, smart.art, 3 (cat), Teerapun, 9 (inset), TessarTheTegu, 12 (inset),
Tony Campbell, 25, Vladimir Melnik, 16, Woody Pope, 3 (squirrel)

Design Elements
Shutterstock: dcwcreations, foxie, happykanppy, JohnySima, jumpingsack, Michal
Ninger, sdecoret

Printed in the United States of America in Stevens Point, Wisconsin.
032013   007227WZF13

TABLE OF CONTENTS

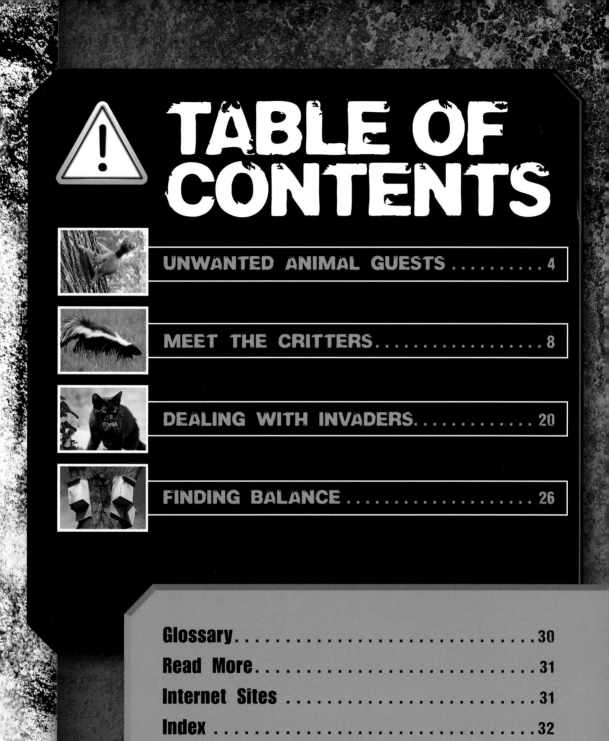

CHAPTER ONE
UNWANTED ANIMAL GUESTS

They squeak and squeal from behind the walls. They raid our cupboards. They leave their droppings in kitchen drawers and behind dishwashers. It's an **infestation** of mice!

Animals that are cute in the wild become less so when they invade our space. Squirrels and other rodents gnaw on electrical wires, causing fires. Mice and rats **contaminate** our food and spread disease. Skunks stink up our homes and cause damage from digging. Bats move into our attics.

The critters aren't trying to cause people harm. They're simply looking for food, water, and shelter to survive. To a squirrel or raccoon, a chimney might seem like a good sleeping place. To a skunk, the space under someone's deck might look like the perfect spot to nest. To a bat, someone's attic might be the right place to make a home.

Invaders Fact
Pet dogs and cats are often the first to notice wild animals that invade homes. They often sniff or paw at the walls where a rodent is lurking.

Mice will feed on bread, fruit, and any other food that is left out for them to find.

infestation—a group of pests that can cause damage or harm

contaminate—to make dirty or unfit for use

Raccoon paw prints

You hear rustling and scraping noises overhead. Could there be ghosts in the attic? Burglars on the roof? No, some kind of animal has invaded your house. But what kind? Just as human criminals leave traces of their whereabouts, so do animal invaders. Different animals leave different clues. You can tell them apart by:

- the sounds they make
- the tracks they create
- the droppings they leave
- the problems they cause

✖ **feces**—poop

✖ **nocturnal**—active at night and resting during the day

For example, squirrels sound different from mice when they make noise. Instead of squeaking, they make growling or screeching noises. Sometimes people hear them rolling nuts on the floor. Squirrels leave tracks with four clawed toes in the front and five in the back. Their **feces** are shaped like chili beans. Squirrels cause problems by making messes and gnawing on wires.

Some home invaders create bigger problems than others. The nature of the crime depends on the critter.

⚠️ GARBAGE PARTY

Raccoons often break into people's garbage. They'll chew through rubber barrels that hold garbage. They'll even prowl through barrels sprinkled with hot sauce. The best way to keep raccoons out of your trash is to put out garbage in the morning. By then, the **nocturnal** animals won't be wandering around.

● Raccoons are excellent climbers. They can scale fences to reach food sources.

CHAPTER TWO

MEET THE CRITTERS

The smell of a skunk can make people wrinkle their noses in disgust. Skunks can release a stinky spray when they feel threatened. Before they spray they give fair warning by stomping their front feet, hissing, and twisting the back of their body in the enemy's direction. Skunks deserve credit for keeping rodent and insect populations in check. However, they may spray or bite people and pets. They also might carry the rare rabies virus. If a skunk has rabies, it may look like it is foaming at the mouth because it has extra saliva. Even if a skunk looks tame, leave it alone. Wild animals can be hard to predict!

RABIES

People bitten by certain animals run the risk of catching the deadly rabies virus. The disease is carried in the saliva of bats, skunks, dogs, and other animals that have the virus. In the United States most dogs are **vaccinated** against rabies. However, this is not the case in other parts of the world. Worldwide more than 99 percent of human rabies deaths come from dogs. People bitten by a type of animal known to carry rabies should go to the doctor right away.

SKUNK

Break-in method: burrowing under house or deck

Evidence: musky odor

Crimes: spraying pets, possibly carrying rabies

✖ **vaccinate**—to give a shot that protects against disease

BAT

Break-in method: entering through gaps in roof overhangs and doors

Evidence: stains from droppings and urine

Crimes: can carry rabies or other diseases

For a female bat, a person's attic is the perfect nursery. It's just the right temperature to raise her young. Bats usually look for places to give birth in the spring. Sometimes people hear the young bats scratching or squeaking.

Bats can live in people's houses for years without them knowing it. The bats' droppings can seep through the attic, staining the walls and ceilings below. The droppings can cause a flulike illness that's mild and curable. A couple of bat species can carry the rabies virus.

Invaders Fact

One bat can eat between 500 and 1,000 mosquitoes in an hour.

× **species**—a group of living things that share characteristics

SQUIRREL

Break-in method: climbing from tree branches into attics

Evidence: scampering noises, damage to electrical wires

Crimes: damage to wires that may cause electrical fires

Homeowners usually hear the gnawing, scratching, and pattering sounds of squirrels in the attic. These bushy-tailed rodents sneak inside to raise their young. During daylight hours squirrels scamper outside to gather nuts. But once inside, squirrels can gnaw on electrical wires, causing fires.

Some squirrels nest in people's cars. Drivers have found nuts and leaves stuffed under the hood of the car. In 2011 a man in Longmont, Colorado, had his car go up in flames. He thought someone was trying to kill him. In fact, a squirrel had made its nest with paper, which had caught fire from the engine's heat.

RACCOON

Break-in method: entering through openings in chimneys, attics, and windows

Evidence: noisy chortling, handprintlike tracks

Crimes: biting pets, possibly carrying rabies and other diseases, gnawing that can cause electrical fires

Invaders Fact

In Brooklyn, New York, raccoons made the news in August 2010 by sneaking into people's kitchens and dining rooms.

Raccoons look like the masked bandits they often are. These determined critters can break into attics by ripping off roof shingles. Once in the attic, they sometimes cause fires by chewing on electrical wires. Raccoons also set up dens in chimneys and beneath porches and decks.

Raccoons pile their new droppings on top of the old, forming dumping grounds called latrines. These nocturnal critters can carry the rabies virus and **parasites** such as roundworm. People—especially young children—can get sick from breathing in roundworm eggs from raccoon feces. One piece of raccoon poop can carry from a few thousand to more than 10 million roundworm eggs.

✗ **parasite**—an animal or plant that lives on or inside another animal or plant

RAT

Break-in method: squeezing through quarter-sized holes

Evidence: smudge marks from body oils, rod-shaped droppings, sounds in walls and attics

Crimes: contaminating food, biting, spreading disease, gnawing that can cause electrical fires

Rats are determined creatures. If they are looking for food or shelter, they can gnaw through wood, sneak through holes, or even get into toilets through sewer pipes. Rats are smart, **adaptable** critters. They need just 1 ounce (28 grams) of food and 0.5 fluid ounce (15 milliliters) of water a day to survive.

Throughout history, disease-carrying rats have killed millions of people. In the Middle Ages (about 500–1500), bubonic plague killed at least one-third of the population of Europe. Rats contributed to the spread of the disease by carrying fleas in their fur. The fleas, in turn, carried plague-causing bacteria. The fleas bit humans and spread the disease.

✖ **adaptable**—able to change when faced with a new situation

MOUSE

Break-in method: squeezing through dime-sized holes

Evidence: scampering sounds inside walls, rod-shaped droppings smaller than those of rats

Crimes: contaminating food, spreading disease, gnawing that can cause electrical fires

Mice are smaller than rats, but they can be just as troublesome. They leave rod-shaped droppings in drawers, shelves, and countertops. They breed so quickly that six mice can become 60 in 90 days.

Mice can live on crumbs, getting most of the water they need from their food. They tear apart pillows, mattresses, and stacks of magazines. They use the gathered materials for their nests. These small rodents gnaw on electrical wires and spread diseases. Mice contaminate 10 times more food than they eat.

DEALING WITH INVADERS

There is a constant battle going on between humans and the furry creatures that invade their homes. Yet many people want to get rid of the critters in a way that is safe for them and the animals.

Knowing what various animals like and dislike is the key to getting them out of a home. The best solutions depend on the animal and the situation. Solutions include scaring them away, trapping them, relocating them, and preventing their invasion in the first place. But you should never try to take care of an infestation on your own. If you find a pesky critter in your home, tell an adult right away.

SCARING THEM AWAY

Sometimes the easiest way to get rid of a pesky critter is to scare it away. Many animals have a strong sense of smell. If exposed to a smell they don't like, the animals may leave. Mice dislike the smell of peppermint. Raccoons scamper away when they get a whiff of garlic.

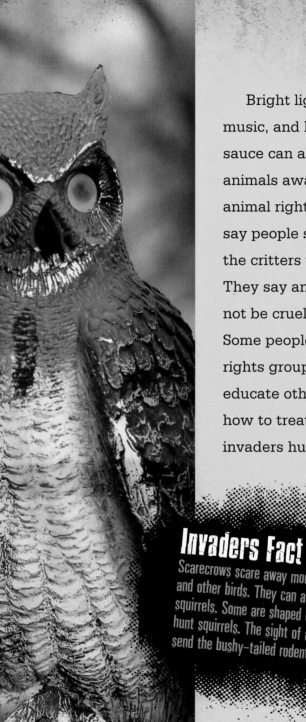

Bright lights, loud music, and hot pepper sauce can also drive animals away. However, animal rights leaders say people should treat the critters with respect. They say animals should not be cruelly scared. Some people in animal rights groups work to educate others about how to treat animal invaders humanely.

Invaders Fact

Scarecrows scare away more than just crows and other birds. They can also frighten off squirrels. Some are shaped like animals that hunt squirrels. The sight of a fake owl can send the bushy-tailed rodents scurrying away.

TRAPS

Some animals are hard to get out of the house. They might need to be trapped instead. But they should be captured in a safe way. The Humane Society of the United States considers glue boards and other deadly traps **inhumane**.

Some traps are meant to capture the invaders alive so they can be released outdoors. For example, a rat can be trapped by placing food in a cage that closes after the rat enters. Then the rat can be released outdoors at least 300 feet (91 meters) from the building.

• Mesh wire cages are traps that are safe for both humans and animals.

In 2011 new rules passed by the U.S. Environmental Protection Agency took effect. Rat poison sold in stores needs to be in special boxes to protect children and pets from harm. However, **exterminators** can still use the old types of poison. People continue to search for new, natural forms of animal control.

RELOCATION

After an animal has been trapped, the next step is to relocate it. The animal can be safely moved to a location that benefits both the person and the animal. However, wildlife experts say that moving animals can cause them harm. Mothers can be separated from their young. Relocating animals takes them away from their familiar sources of food, water, and shelter. Some animals die as a result. A licensed wildlife rehabilitator can help in these situations. A wildlife rehabilitator is someone who cares for injured, sick, or orphaned wild animals.

✖ **inhumane**—describes actions that are cruel or unkind
✖ **exterminator**—a person who rids places of unwanted pests for a living

PREVENTION

Take away the access to food, water, and shelter animal invaders need, and they're forced to look elsewhere. Animals become familiar with the houses in their neighborhoods. Raccoons can lift off the rubber seals around plumbing vents and sneak inside. If the vents are covered with animal-proof screening, the raccoons will move on. Homeowners can also plug up holes, cap their chimneys, and fix broken windows and doors.

Often people attract wild animals with their garbage. Putting garbage in animal-proof barrels can send the creatures sniffing somewhere else for food.

Critters also munch on pet food and feces. Storing pet food in closed containers and cleaning up your pet's feces can help keep away unwanted animals.

Invaders Fact

Squirrels and raccoons sometimes sneak in through pet doors. Pet doors can be made to only open for your pet. These doors respond to a signal on the pet's collar.

● Leaving pet food outside may attract wild animals.

25

CHAPTER FOUR
FINDING BALANCE

Living in balance with nature takes hard work. Careful planning for the future involves limiting the pain and suffering of animals and changing some of our own behaviors.

In some cases, people are moving into animals' **habitats**. When new houses and buildings are built, they can take over the area where animals once lived. The animals may try to find new homes in the new buildings. That's why prevention is important. It's easier to keep the critters out right away than try to get rid of them after they've invaded.

All animals are part of an **ecosystem**. They interact with the environment and other animals. That's one reason why experts say it's important to deal with pesky critters in a humane way. For example, if all the rats in a certain area are killed, animals that eat rats will have less food. Then those animals might start to die out unless they find another food source.

BRILLIANT WHITE

INDOOR/OUTDOOR

PAINTABLE

FLEXIBLE

EASY WATER CLEAN-UP

Wo

Pene

● Mice can sneak into garages and build nests among the tools and supplies.

✳ **habitat**—the natural place and conditions in which a plant or animal lives

✳ **ecosystem**—a system of living and nonliving things in an environment

• Bat boxes help both humans and bats. Bats use the boxes as homes, so they aren't as likely to invade houses.

Scientific breakthroughs could make life easier for humans and furry invaders. In Davis, California, researchers are working on a way to help farmers protect their fields from squirrels. A medicine could prevent squirrels from having babies. Fewer squirrels would mean fewer problems.

Some people would rather use the squirrels' own enemies to control them. Hawks, for example, kill and eat squirrels. While hawks and other rare animals are protected by wildlife protection laws, other animals are not. Animal control laws vary from state to state. In many states, bats cannot be harmed. Mice and rats, on the other hand, can be killed or captured.

Preventing critters from invading buildings is a challenge. New solutions are needed to keep both people and animals safe. Prevention and humane methods of pest control can help people and animals live in balance.

Invaders Fact

Anti-cruelty laws are starting to apply to animals long considered pests. Someone who kills a skunk with a bow and arrow, for instance, might be charged with animal cruelty.

GLOSSARY

adaptable (uh-DAP-ta-buhl)—able to change when faced with a new situation

contaminate (kuhn-TA-muh-nayt)—to make dirty or unfit for use

ecosystem (EE-koh-sis-tuhm)—a system of living and nonliving things in an environment

exterminator (ik-STUHR-muh-nay-tuhr)—a person who rids places of unwanted pests for a living

feces (FEE-cees)—poop

habitat (HAB-uh-tat)—the natural place and conditions in which an animal or plant lives

infestation (in-fes-TAY-shun)—a group of pests that can cause damage or harm

inhumane (IN-hyoo-mayn)—describes actions that are cruel or unkind

nocturnal (nok-TUR-nuhl)—active at night and resting during the day

parasite (PAIR-uh-site)—an animal or plant that lives on or inside another animal or plant

vaccinate (VAK-suh-nayt)—to give a shot that protects against disease

READ MORE

Carney, Elizabeth. *Bats.* Washington, D.C.: National Geographic, 2010.

Day, Trevor. *Secret Life of Rats: Rise of the Rodents.* Extreme! Mankato, Minn.: Capstone Press, 2009.

Diemer, Lauren. *Squirrels.* Backyard Animals. New York: Weigl Publishers, 2008.

Read, Tracy. *Exploring the World of Raccoons.* Buffalo, N.Y.: Firefly Books, 2010.

INTERNET SITES

FactHound offers a safe, fun way to find Internet sites related to this book. All of the sites on FactHound have been researched by our staff.

Here's all you do:

Visit *www.facthound.com*

Type in this code: 9781476501413

Super-cool stuff! Check out projects, games and lots more at
www.capstonekids.com

INDEX